POEMS FOR MARIA: Blue Fire

POEMS FOR MARIA: Blue Fire

Stanley Gemmell

Library of Congress Control Number:		2023915762
ISBN:	Hardcover	979-8-3694-0581-9
	Softcover	979-8-3694-0582-6
	eBook	979-8-3694-0583-3

Print information available on the last page.

Rev. date: 08/17/2023

To order additional copies of this book, contact:
Xlibris
844-714-8691
www.Xlibris.com
Orders@Xlibris.com
552135

Dedicated to Maria Talanova

CONTENTS

PREFACE

I have been warned that love is real. That souls are not to be toyed with and above all, that one's own, very Being relies upon love for *existence*. I believe all of this, but certainly do not understand it. I try my best to, however. Since I have had awareness, I have loved love. I remember fantasizing at age 6 about kissing Shirley Temple, my pillow held in my loving embrace, my face smushing kisses onto it. I believe that love should be free. I don't believe in legislating it. I don't believe in collectively scorning it. I lament current world views denigrating so many of the various kinds and modes of love. For me, being amarous and romantic is simply part of my nature. It would break my heart if I were not free to follow my heart.

I am not cupiditous. I am a very loyal partner. I value my companion so much that it is a joy for me to continually prove it. I apologize to every person in my life who has ever felt let down by me, for any reason, regarding romance. I happen to be a man, I happen to be in love with a woman, and this book is not about *getting* her, although I pray she always enjoys reading it. I pray Maria never becomes my enemy. Love can turn to hate. I thank goodness this has never happened to me. I wheel and deal as very much I can, behind the scenes, to help prevent this possibility from ever manifesting.

I have never yet, personally, met Maria Talanova. The emotions and thoughts generated by her grew, organically, from admiring her social media; and also from receiving approbation and support from her (and others) for my efforts.

I would like to thank all of the people who have supported or tolerated my 39 years as a poet. This is my first book. I began to write it after experiencing a technical crisis in which I thought my internet cloud infrastructure had vanished, leaving me bereft of hundreds of pages of creative materiel. I have kept my usual quirk: I sign every poem after its completion. My pen name of Stanley Gemmell is in honor of my step-father, John Gemmell, who brought me up in the Arthurian, Chivalric Tradition. My greatest Patron is my mother, Anna Velicer.

I hope you enjoy this book and I also hope that you read it aloud. Anything you hear or think regarding it is *valid*. There are no hidden meanings or secret codes in it, other than the wondrous capacities of *language* itself.

Thank You For Your Time,

Stanley Gemmell

August 2, 2023 - 2:32 AM - Las Olas, Ft. Lauderdale

*NOTE REGARDING THIS TEXT: All distortions are completely intentional.

My life consists of two moments: number 1 moment was yesterday's yesterday when I saw an alexandrine mermaid swim, she adjusted her hair and had every detail same as folks in air, she looked away only to truly look There, exactly where you After her look Will Have been | moment number 2 was today when I saw her spin and take even the hint or perhaps rarest trace of a step in my direction <--> These moments give me the strength to handle the destinies of this day, to settle old friends' hearts who now decide to treat me differently, I accept, I smile, I may or may not give a small bow since I show my regard, and not my submission <--> real friendship charges more than the other can pay, to make it look more real for Everyone: the rich are honored for their actions, the ones left out have more time to make unique offerings: remember that BOTH are priceless, no need to discriminate, we all share one purpose, to eliminate unkind judgements

FRAGMENT FOR SUNG PRAISES
S t a n l e y G e m m e l l
July 10, 2023

BLUE FLAME FIRE (SEQUENCE IN THREE PARTS)

FIRST PART:
Blue fire, the thought that the water thought to make love,
My eyes grew clouded from bliss they hardened into sharp
Jewels but expanded back into their own abyss
From which you emerged, dripping spinning planets
And the single, funerary comet which travels
In the counter-direction to all the rest,
"Sigh," you told me, "you'll be waiting
Long for me to return, we have only this once
To again and again urge, the other from bliss
To greater love and thought regarding such.
Therefore, sigh... for you, it is good therapy."
My mind knew not to wander, for once, of course,
Stunned, my only job was to avoid disbelief.
Impossible, I thought to myself, I thought I
Had heard the word being said, such an impossible
Word to say, at a time like this. She let brown
Hair touch her shoulder (touched by wind) before
She lightly brushed it back.

STANLEY GEMMELL
7/7/2023

SECOND PART:

Blue fire, the thought that the water thought to make life,
My mind grew clouded from love they softened into warm
And salted pools but expanded up into clouds their own heaven
From which you emerged, refreshed and sparkling and singing
The single, sacred, silent, all-pervasive musical note of joy.
Being had paused, the transformation of the cosmos
Took only an instant, and afterward, everything
Became permanently immanent: it existed
Within itself as well as outside of itself.
I heard your voice speak,
"What you term life is actually death.
The prison you call flesh prevents you from yourself.
But only because greater things are being prepared
For your return, so that the longer you live, the greater
Your reward. You should smile, although it is hard.
You should rejoice, although you feel to weep.
These contradictions are roving signs.
They, like yourself, are Truth's Keep!"
I closed my eyes and saw a great kilonova.
A dense, grey, neutron star exploding into a black hole.
An aura of blue flame mixed into the silence,
Since things in space are rarely heard.

STANLEY GEMMELL
7/7/2023 2nd of 3 blue flame sequences

THIRD PART:

Blue as sky and ocean
Hot like hope or fear
Fire fills the crystal
Worn behind her
Forehead, the jewel
Of her mind that seethes
Like an engine of
The divine switched
On to reveal
The inner workings
Of mankind, to her
Eyes alone.

In the astral
Heavenly plains
This blue, fiery
Jewel is a dragon's egg
Which hatches galaxies
And as each new, spinning
World creates another,
The dragon's talons extend.

The screens and offices,
Schedules and rituals
Of our world attend.

In the breaths of woman
And man.

———————————

———————————

STANLEY GEMMELL
7/8/2023 3rd of 3 blue flame poems <3

POEM BY NATURE (WRIT OF YELLOW TOPAZ)

mermaid of yellow topaz

A mermaid of shifting, cut, yellow Topaz

An origin at dance with the center with no name

Because to speak it would never end

A water tiger girl near a submerged
shaft of sunlight that sought her
happy company

Because to speak it would never end
The matter regarding in what fine manner
The beam of light had first visited Cool Tree
And drunk its shade before penetrating
The surface of the clear, azure-hued
    pool oh very sweetly
   did the shaft of sunlight
dip itself, neatly, not
seeming to disturb
the liquid

Night fell, everything, even the sun itself,

Had forgotten about the sun beam, who

Chuckled, very pleased to have spent

So much time playing and dancing

With the five leafed Topaz gleaming

Tiger lily water girl, who

Listened to its life story

With candid and rapt

Attention, the liquid

Playing Host to this strange meeting

Was also quite entranced and enthused.

What could it mean? That such a rare

And lucky meeting had taken place

Without anybody planning it, or,

Ever having been able to foresee ?

"No matter," the girl shrugged, "sunbeams

Never tire, they are warm and happy by nature,

I have made a friend, the light ray said

That it would meet me at Cool Tree

Two days after first snow, to let

The frost better settle, and I

Have memorized what it looks like --"

"Exactly," the beam broke in, happy

To mischievously interrupt her, "sunbeams
Never tire, we are very subtle and beautiful --"

"By nature." She returned the mischievous favor.
The sunbeam smiled, then continued, "I plan upon
Visiting many awesome places to gather rich fables
To relate to her --"

"After he arrives." She explained. The shaft of light
Seemed touched and gladdened, then said, "Although,
We are neither a he, nor a she."

Just a piece of the impossible
Doing impossible things, all day.
A clasp of comet's tail to shed light like wisdom
Itself because it has a precise vector, like wisdom.
Love for life begins this world, but must outlast it.
A friend for the submerged. The silence that yielded
My self who saw it, although it could easily have been you.
A faithful, constant companion, whom all wish to talk to,
& give their report of what had happened & what they saw.

_____

_____

Stanley Gemmell
7/8/2023

One day, the world was saved by a beautiful woman
Asleep inside the dream of a pool within a cave
Whose roof was splashed with white sparks and stars
The next day, the world being saved, you offered me
To look at one of either two things, whose nature
You would not reveal until I had made the choice
Either Near or Far...

I struggled with this, I thought, if I choose Near
She may only offer me that which I know
That I may approach ... But if I choose Far
Who knows if all I will receive is just the
Opposite of what I am able to take

I awoke from the dream with water upon my face
All during the night I had wept and wept,
Oh Savage World, to offer such a choice
Between what I may have or what I can want!

———————

———————

THE CHOICE
Stanley Gemmell
7/9/2023

●●●●●●●●●●●●●●●●●●●●●●●●●●●●●●●●●●●●

*** All Paths Lead To Love***

●●●●●●●●●●●●●●●●●●●●●●●●●●●●●●●●●

Desire has become my master
For the sake of your goodness
And that of God's
I clutch four roses at my breast
One for you One for me
One for Them & One for Him
All paths lead to Love

The thing that I want is you
Although it rains in the crowded
Heaven of your look

I may breathe my best hopes
As you dance the sun
Into my brain

I may sweeten the air
With my laughter

But you are the one thing that remains
The same, day in and day out,
Perfection

One day, death will find me
As if inside a giant
Egg of white light

Perhaps we will converse
Perhaps not, but if so
I'll smile & give thanks

Because in that moment
That I first saw you
Nothing mattered;

But ever since,
Everything has.

All things did matter most, before
This moment. Love told me once,
Before ruining my life, that a perfect
Thing existed, but I refused to believe.

I guess Desire is a good master, though,
I shrug. Because it is the one thing
Capable of creating joy out of disaster.
You will only ever want what's best for you,

Always, already, no matter who says what.
And with that premise alone, everyone agrees!

_____

_____

POEM WITH LOVE
Stanley Gemmell
7/9/2023

NOTHING SATISFIES, NOTHING YIELDS

except for your notice, your
attention ... something eludes me,
everything evades ... only hunger
is my advantage; only hope & thirst.

I keep my wits about me,
as happiness in life slips just
out of my range, I struggle
forward, feeling the weight
& pressure of the stars &
heavenly bodies of the spheres
above, I pray to Existence for
The power of surprise & survival

What shall prove me to myself
& what can ever prove my self
To you? Like giants made of
Fire & Ice my eyes glaze over
In combat with both time & want.

Only the salted ocean soothes me.
Only the waves at my breast.

———————————

———————————

STANLEY GEMMELL
7/9/2023

THE WAY I CRY IS NOT UNUSUAL

Nor the things I cry about
My eyes well up, then I tremble
Fear and hope and un-space mix
I feel trapped but in the act of escaping
I struggle to forget why it is I am crying
Even as I celebrate and rejoice in it
I push and pull against what should be
With what is and is even now, still
Nothing has stopped
Everything is sped up
But nothing moves faster
Except my relief, because
I know two things:
That something has happened
And that this means something begins

—————————

—————————

STANLEY GEMMELL
7/8/2023

SONG FOR PRESENT FUTURE LOVE

When you are too scared to think about tomorrow
For fear you will not make the most out of today

The apocalypse is a spectrum, it is asked,
Upon which where it is that one fits in

If you were gone, my landscape would be empty
Of hope for anything to hold, which meant more
than what ever could be told

To bravely face the gaze of life
And maintain poise before uncertainty
As colors flare wildly, and gravity shakes the sky
The forgotten memories of the touch of the hand
cannot be left too far behind

Oh, love of this moment, forever and all time
Say you will stay, again and again, even if there
be nothing at all that is ever left remaining except
you and I

STANLEY GEMMELL

7/11/2023

**SO HAPPY SO PLEASED A GREAT BIG SMILE
FOR YOUR LOVELY STYLE AND GRACE ... YOU
ARE LIKE A GIANT SUNFLOWER DRINKING
THE SOLAR RAYS TILTING YOUR HEAD AND
BODY IN THE SWEET-SCENTED WIND**

The gaze of your eyes has changed me
To look at the human face, for me,
Shall never be the same

Again and again, you astound me,
You frighten me, because you
Change but stay the same

Who are you to recreate beauty
When truth is beauty
And beauty truth

For me what is most wild
Is this savage love

No one else I know has ever cared
As much
`````````` as you
``````````

But cared even more to contain it,
To shape it, and to tame it,
To help it to stay true

_____

_____

STANLEY GEMMELL
JULY 12, 2023

AN OFFER OF FOOD AS A POEM

Fearlessly scan within and without for difference
Then bravely withstand each and every detail

One will notice sad things, yes, of course, yet
Greater still one will notice the greatness of Hope

Insofar, to the extent, toward the limit of what may Be
One raises one's hands for silence or else for glee

Both ways matter, both ways feed
The ebb and fiber of our oceans
and the veins of our leaves

Interconnecting vibrancy
Tiny, locking, unlocking
circles and slants

Form shivering diamonds
And squares and tri-angled wholes

Of melting and dripping and reforming hues
Reds into Yellows into Oranges and dark Blues

Or else rich vermillions and shiny or matte pastels
Streak upon the vision like dancing, jumping, shaking
(s)elves

The singer of songs offers wisdom
By invisible means, to hearts

Not fattened Nor softened Nor too-lean Or too-mean
An offer of food as poem, will feed the starved
& lame & blind

With visions of salt oceans and fields of tall rye
And with eyes closed and the pursed lips of a smile

Return light for light and truth for truth
And linger after long whiles

_____

_____

STANLEY GEMMELL
7/12/2023

Today I made a tomb for two friends out of a giant pine cone. They are both insects: very fine Blattodea, used to being undervalued. Me? I am so grateful that about 19 years ago I found myself surrounded by a circus of them, doing tricks and teaching me their Sacred Lore. Ever since, I have learned so much: they can live for twenty days after their head has been chopped off, they have infrared sensors in their butts, I saw one I had given a tiny hunk of cheese to (massive to his proportions, I bet) basically make love to the thing as it happily devoured it <-- the hunk of cheese I mean | but the best of all is that if there is no male around, the women will still procreate. These are facts, as impossible as it seems, that I made a petition to get folks to sign, just to say that they oppose the murder of them. I made a kind of Friendly Mascot Picture - the Blattodea was smiling - I had hoped for signatures, but I guess too many fear to honor what they might mistakenly think superior. What does this have to do with ultimate beauty, magical grace, and the utmost of dire Truth? Why, everything, of course... we all share One Earth <3

POEM IN PRAISE OF THE BEAUTY IN ALL SENTIENT LIFE

(Using A Beautiful Model As Emblem Of Hope & Grace)
STANLEY GEMMELL
JULY 10, 2023

THE LIGHTNING AND THE EMERALD

About two weeks ago I attempted to visit what I consider my grandmother's grave. It is not where she is actually buried, but instead the house where she finally lived. The house was set into the side of the hill, the roof of the place was where we parked our cars. And beneath and behind it lay the yard. When I was very little I saw many wonders there: giant turtles and lowing cows, bulls with long horns, and at night the sky was full of stars, and the yellow and oblong moon. But when I turned the vehicle onto the road to arrive there, it began to suddenly rain. With a fearsome force and many frightening and loud crashes of vivid and bright yellow lightning. I feared for my life, it was so sudden and steep, the wall of energy and shakings and rain; the bottomless well of grey. I turned back around and nearly instantly, the rain disappeared, as if it were never there.

Maybe twelve hours ago, or so, I held my emerald in my mouth. I rolled its slick beauty along my teeth and tongue (it helps me think, it helps me be) and my best friend, unknown to me... was in a mood. I was ranting some foul mouthed hatred upon a supposed foe, someone who had stolen poetry from me, but that story is very old. I was sitting at the edge of my bed, my face was looking down, and the emerald slipped from my tongue, but I never heard it hit the ground. I figured it had landed upon my lap, or somewhere near the bed, I spent hours and hours looking for my bright green thing. It had done this once before, gone from the second floor to the first. I thought it was a miracle then, but not like this time, just now. When about four hours ago I saw it three feet SouthWest of where it was to land. Plain as day and still bright green, nothing about it hid.

Between the windows of the sea, behind the mirror of the sun, it had gathered secretly, with the One of whom I love. I imagine her left side pocket, just inside her hip, a magic dimple of sun-shine-lit..

What were they discussing in the sacred space of dreams. Were her eyes slowly watering, at what it means to feel? Are lightning and the emerald really the same thing?

Are tears just strange and frozen crystals, fallen from the crowns of kings? My holy wishes fill my head. I am sure of just one thing: that never again shall I fear to tread, where only angels sing.

——————————

——————————

STANLEY GEMMELL
JULY 13, 2023

TWO HOUR SHOCK - A SHORT FORM DIALOGUE

The Violet-Rich Muse:
"My loveley beggar here-in Audient
Mine, my Belovet & unfoolish one
Forever not-thou, & Forever ours
Mine, my bravest one, Oh, mine, mine
Mine my happy, endless one"

The Bard-Cleric-Mage Knight:
"For one lock of your hair has fallen
To me to keep, I sleep the Risen Sun"

She:
"Explain"

He:
"I sang a song of prayer to the Earth
The Moon & The Stars, then slept;
Upon arising to my amazement
About the handle of my long-sword
Was coiled Thirteen strands of your
Precious hair; I heard the horn sound
And would have missed the field

Were it not for the Nighting-Gale,
The Loggerhead-Shrike,
& the Columbidae had sang
In Unison for me to Awake.
Since it is a strict requirement
Of my Order to heed the Call
Of both love and Song,
I held to the honor of Belief."

She:
"I am relieved"

He:
"I will regale you further with a secret
Regards toward Age-ing, That & That
The eyes must be retrained by
Force of loss of habit in their Strength,
That & That, the mind is thus Further
Retrained."

She:
"I gain focus regularly"

He:
"And as for the locks of your merit-drenched hair,
They were fused to the handle of my long-sword."

She:

"I am again assured"

He:

"There are no requirements regarding
The fresh and the cool of the night,
Neither are there any for the waves
Of the sea, or treasure-rich caves,
Or meadows, or even forests.
All is permitted the sanity of joy,
And to these you must invite yourself."

THESE EVENTS TRANSPIRED DURING
A TWO HOUR TIME-SPAN OF RECORDED
BLACK-WAVE ACTIVITY, MEASURED AS
GREEN-FUSCHIA ARCS SPERSED WITH
ALTERNATE WHITE-GREY PULSES

———————————

———————————

STANLEY GEMMELL
July 13, 2023

VOLCANO OF BEAUTY (THE TORNADO RAINBOW)

Sweet Dolce Yum, how have the waters
grown? Inside a small, spinning vortex
of rain and wind, that can step lightly
over some things, upon others pounce,
do the bright colors blend? Or else,
somehow do they just shake & bounce?
Sweet Dolce Yum, you have powder
on your face. You joined the human race.
People wonder like-what it tastes.
Beige and pink and pale face,
Curled into a ball of praise,
Or sometimes scorn.
Sweet Dolce Yum, I will tell you.
Sweet Dolce Yum, I will tell you
What I think of this; what I think of you:
"I agree with what is said by most,
that it is better to look upon the sun
for one or two moments, than gaze
too long upon the dark of the moon.
It is better to gaze up at the stars,
Or out over the cooling, rolling sea,
Than to needlessly journey,

Except if it's for love,
Except it be for love."
The colors seep slowly out of the ground,
The top of the volcano shakes then bursts:
A cycling spout of myriad colors is loosed
First, then many more follow in happy volleys.

———————————

———————————

STANLEY GEMMELL
July 13, 2023

Rich tressed Nemesis was indignant that her Father the King of the Gods, wished to lie with her. In her heart she heard another calling for her love. This explains why a Good Father gives the daughter away at the marriage feast, but (this) does not explain her indignation. A wild woman may of course give herself away, and the union suffers nothing as result, perhaps some of the most successful families were formed by orphans. Of course, a normal man shall marvel if he be so lucky as to have helped to give birth to a beautiful woman by providing his esteemed wife the factor of his seed, and every culture agrees to this, since it is better to search far and wide, if one is able to and one has that wish, to cultivate a friendship suitable for the ultimate destiny of love. All of this is part of the cycles of nourishment. But kingship is strange and often confuses the man or woman that bears it. Ultimate authority, such that every subject fears to become an advisor, since the great responsibility of failed hopes, or else the fragility of success itself's excellence: may fall short of the exact mark of what's truly needed. In such strained circumstance the king is beset. Trapped by fate to hide the source of merit: excellence; behind the facade of his emblem: the crown. In fact, it was a mad king in France that ruined the nation just before Joan The Maid flourished to save it! All this is to say that Nemesis was right, and her father was not wrong, simply confused and not himself. Nemesis gave birth. Her offspring Helen was the most beautiful thing in the world. Many wars were fought for the prestige and glory and pleasure of her hand. Nemesis watched. As the stories of mankind progressed, so too, did the Gods', whenever and wherever they were successfully remembered. It is said that Nemesis now has a function: it is to cut down the joy of those who possess too much of it. Since the world is still imperfect, and pleasure and happiness leads weak souls to boast and to exult, and to forget that for every victor, there lies the defeated, whether or not it is ever actually deserved.

ANOTHER CALL FOLDED INTO THE WINGS OF A GODDESS

Stanley Gemmell

July 14, 2023

I think about her all the time
Sunlight or dark make no sense
My mind searches feelings
My heart refuses to rhyme

Food is incidental
Simply fuel for
Another, "I love you."
I wonder if I am sane.

Walking like a panther
Among drumbeats
And guitars that form
The body of a woman,

I still tie down my soul
I hold my tongue
I actually pray
I have never cared before

.Carved kisses in the deeps
Of blue and olive bodies
Of water

I would notice if I was crying
If I were not busy smiling
Because the laughter wells
From an innocent sigh

;from her, a flare of
the hips, or a haughty
work of purest art,
an arpeggio, or
gargantuan scale.

Surely, love is the theme
An entire series of Ages
Had foretold because it
Had foreseen.

———————————

———————————

PEOPLE SEE A CAREFREE MAN
Stanley Gemmell
July 14, 2023

Fair Lady, I devote myself to you
Ceaselessly cleansing myself of fear

Your magnificent charm is worthy
Of my every possible thought or deed

The goodness you embody
Is like the moon, it is pale and soft

If I were to see you blush
The face of the sky would rose

If I were to know your breath
My soul fills with hot-house flowers

Oh that your heart beat faster
At the sound of my name!

With pleasure and delight
To view your humble servant

Who begs the entire world in your name
To help him be able to keep his eyes raised

TO AVOID DESPAIR

Stanley Gemmell - July 14, 2023

TEARS OF SPRING

The girl holds a cluster of red grapes
In her right hand, before her face
And in her left, a cluster of green
Grapes to her ear, there are red
And green grapes in her hair,
Her garment is dyed with
The green blood of emeralds,
Her upper chest is bare and visible.
Outside it is summer,
Watered by spring's tears,
The years having been made visible
As the clouds slowly near a procession:
I have found a description of the event:
"The girl actually had held a cluster
of red grapes to her right cheek
in an earlier Painted Sky. What
the usual myths rely upon is
the narrator voice, however,
it is an error to assume the poet
is in full awareness of each prior
circumstance, since creation
does not always partake of history.

Being familiar with this matter,
I suggest that the focus remain
upon the procession, and not
the icon. For instance: it is said
that the icon wears a garment
stained with the blood of an
emerald, and this is true, yet
an often forgotten detail is
that the emerald is continuously
bled During the procession
and that the blood is ritually
watered with sunlight in order
for the garment to better stain.
This is why both garment and jewel
are Lime color green, and not the
typical darker green of what many
think are True Emerald. There are
reasons why the jewel itself is more
active after mixing with sunlight,
and the garment more appealing.
Years of the suppression of the ritual
knowledge of Love-Sacrifice, an art
that requires great subtlety and bravery,
have led to these common errors.
Further, the icon is surrounded by

multi-beasts. Some with the head
of a falcon and body of a bear,
some with the hind legs of frogs
and sex of the feline, some with
fiery wings and metallic, gold skin.
These various configurations
Surround the icon During the procession,
guarding her and re-invigorating her
chosen focus." As a red and white
Spiral hath traced itself upon Her
Cheek, so does the Center of the
Procession also hold, this is to say:
Dually. For there is an invisible
Other forever sharing her space
Although He himself be on the
Other side of the World. It is
Clear that the cycle of the Seasons
Reinforce Themselves as Their Love.

Thusly centered and forever re-centered
In a balance of twin beams, the long
Horizontal look of the Earth meets the Sky
At Horizon. The thin line of tender meeting
Which blends the green of the land or sea

With the red or pink of the sun During
Rise or Set.

_____

_____

FIGURE EIGHT (8) COBWEB OF LIGHTNING

Let the first thing that you see each day
Be the memory of the rolling springs
Beneath the lights where-in you dream
And shadow casts its day

Finally left for welcome
The sea has opened its doors

Beneath its cobwebs of lightning-glass
That shift and reek with wisdoms past
And gathered lovingly into the arms
Of eternal - joined circles[: the warm
earth-core]

Finally left open to welcome
The sea has pulled its shores

The unceasing waves from the center
Of the earth, to rise and touch
the coasts - then wake from
dream like seawaves - a lovely girl
to step-sing lightly - like the foam.

[the cooling sweet liquid]
Our shores of surf to sound the drone,
Gently sun-kissed - her eyelids flutter,
Awake again, to smile, like a rhythmic
Slope of salt washing water,
The look in her eye is
The oldest, blue-green song!

_____

_____

STANLEY GEMMELL
July 14, 2023
*Note: The Numeral (8) of the title is silent
and not meant to be read aloud. The spoken
title should be read to speak:
"Figure eight, cobweb of lightning."

THREE SCENES FROM A HEALING BY FAITH

❀❀❀❀❀

Compulsion after tenderly blotted kingfisher's wing
Duo by sun ❀❀❀❀❀ Drying moss off broken gallows
For transfusion by overlapping wave's froth ❀❀❀❀❀
Spume splattered beaks ❀❀❀❀ Two birds next
The other's perfect alignment ❀❀❀❀❀ House
Of the vast olive face of gentle and undulating
Ocean They The Two Birds Are Flying Next To
❀❀❀❀ Cowrie shells dangle wet dancing To
The touch of the ❀❀❀❀❀ Cooling liquid covers
Such human handfuls of the sand-grains ❀❀❀❀❀
By sand-grains opened human hands ❀❀❀❀❀
Two by two the kingfishers dip Oh nearly touching

The line of honied syrup's sand sight Like two native
Greyed to Steel-Green White horizon's line The Two
Birds form a compass unto themselves Adjacent drips
The ocean Cowrie shells dancing to wet touch of cooling
Liquid covers the vast olive face of gentle and undulating
By sand-grains opening the human hands Two by two
The line of honied kingfishers dip Oh nearly kissing

43

The human enters the ocean green The touch of
Cooling covers Two by two the kingfishers dip Oh
Touching nearly kissing The wing duo by sun Oh
By sand-grains opened human hands Of the vast
Olive face of gentle and undulating
Ocean They The Two Birds Are Flying Next To

———————————

———————————

STANLEY GEMMELL
July 14, 2023

I swam in the Atlantic ocean. I opened my eyes beneath the neon, lime-green water.

The ocean told me: existence demands improvement. I replied: well then, let me prove it.

I imagined my hoped-for / hopeful / lover's wrist, the way she grips the handle of a wheeled case,

The way she threads it through the mighty labyrinth, of this airport, or else, that.

The rest of the people do not take notice. The way folks duck their heads

When forced to walk past a public, live, news broadcast. They, themselves: unhurried:

Blahzey to any and all weather forecasts, in tune to each others' shrugs. At best: amused:

To my poet heart's yearning, for the furnace of my hope's bliss, the fiery cage that

I sear my love upon, the rotisserie spit of my lush and fondest dreams.

The lit faggot whose torch-light I use to see, myself in the mirror, evolving

Into my home-team's image of itself: the mascot for True and Possible Love.

The Atlantic is warm and clean, the beautiful people are gathered, serene.

Every voice abuzz with Stan. The poet's long journey Home:

What's she like: they say. But they don't wait for an answer:
They themselves reply: Her existence needs no improvement.
And I laugh and say: most definitely, no need to prove it.
Her obvious grace sustains entire armies. Men and boys
Vye for the touch of her hand. She is adept at every form
Of nourishment. Her sacred tears water the land.
The beautiful goddess of every sacred good,
Who need not raise her voice to echo the wood.
And I laugh and say: most definitely, no need to prove it.
But my people know me best, and they wink and sigh and say:
Oh, Stanley, do not even think of putting her to the test.
It has been ten days of infinity: she wins every time: you tried
your best!

THE SUBMERGED POET ALLOWS SAND TO SLIP FROM HIS FINGERS

Stanley Gemmell

July 14, 2023

Notes: "Blahzey" is American Slang for "Indifferent" or "Contented disinterest" *

A "faggot" is a bundle of thin sticks lit to make a torch, also a pejorative (dirty) word for "homosexual man" * A "rotisserie" is a rotating spit used to cook meat over fire, or hot coals * To "vye" is to "strive for" or "try very hard"

Post Script: To "duck" is slang for "lowering one's head" usually to avoid some thing or gaze

TERROR FOR LOVE

To hear her voice is to feel a hand
upon the soul, an unexpected crash
of massive, brass cymbals, as if
fallen from Mount Kazbek.
Mount Kazbek, in the Caucasus
Mountains, is the place where
Heracles freed the Titan Prometheus
From bondage. Prometheus had
tricked the father of the gods
by giving him the worthless pieces
of meat after animal sacrifice, while
secretly giving humanity the best.
The father shed Wrath and took
Fire from man, but Prometheus,
Undeterred, stole the fire back!
And for this the father forged
The chains at the top of
Christ Mountain Peak,
"the one covered by ice"
Over sixteen-thousand feet high,
A potentially still-active volcano.
To feel her touch although very

Distant is to feel the Eagle the father
Sent to tear out Prometheus' liver
Every day, the violent myth of beauty.
Her image bleeds lime juice upon
Out from the glass that covers it,
One's fingers yearn for the molecules
Responsible for the fragrant citrus.
The constant, giant bird scream
Beautiful in the back of the mind's throat.
It is said that soul itself chooses either
Its heaven, or even its own hell,
And that one need not die to enter it.
But the truth of the story is that all
Of these still burning fires are merely Signals.
One may postpone their meaning,
But never indefinitely.
One must choose the sweet fragrance
Of her body, whether in dream, or physically.
Cross vast distances, although they remain
At arm's reach. The alkaline trachyte
Sheathed in lava, pelted by meteors of olivine.
Seen as a fiery light-show from view of Mount Olympos,
Home of the sublime and serene.
I take scant notice and continue my climb.
Improbably dressed only in thin, white boxer shorts.
The beautiful woman worth far more than sleep,

Or safety. The haunting gaze of her look
Informing my every move. Reaching up
For precarious hand-hooks, dragging my
Thrilling, trembling body higher. Glancing
Down to place my naked toes upon a slant
Of cruel and white-beautiful snow,
The echoes of the music I heard below
Reverberating my torso. The blush
Pink half smile of her tilted face
Ironic and perfect and meaninglessly pure.
She is all the world, and I am never alone!

_____

_____

STANLEY GEMMELL
July 14, 2023

POEM TO COME DOWN THE MOUNTAIN

I had looked up at the wall as a teenage lunatic, zero fear of
death. I saw nothing but a hundred

foot high wall, mostly at a slant. "I got this," I thought, "only
the very last twenty or so feet go

straight up..." I was wearing thin athletic shorts and a white
t shirt, I think it had read,

"I Survived 1993" and had a French Renaissance engraving
theme, sweetly complex

(it made the eyes rhyme) ... I started up. I was like a monkey
climbing a palm.

My two knees gripped the craggy wall's sides, at the geometric,
triangular slant that it formed.

The fortress loomed large, of very-course, but to me it seemed
small. I was about sixty feet high

up, or so, before I began to feel fear. The wind whipped so
much louder, the incline had most

subtly decreased its sharpness, it seemed that little by little, I
was forced to go More straight up!

My legs began to tremble from the energy I had exerted, and
sweat ran from my brow into my

eyes. I suppressed even the notion of panic. But the wind
raged harder, at the coast of the

frighteningly deep ocean, and I began to have some doubts...
in order to re-adjust my climb,

I was forced to glance down. For those three or four seconds,
everything slowed down, the

green grass below swam wildly up and down. I took my
chances and decided that up was less

scary than down! By my estimation, I was more than two-
thirds high up into my climb. But only

two or three pulls up and my body completely rebelled. The
wind did not relent, I knew that

I was defeated in my intention, I only wished to survive! I
clutched the craggy nooks of the fierce,

dark, brown castle walls and moved my right thigh slightly
down. And that's when it hit me: this

wall was exactly Designed for this! The second one leg let go
of its clutch against the fortress side,

my entire body felt vertigo and was forced to push harder into
the wall to retain its grip.

I knew I was very possibly finished. I was forced first to calm
down, my heart-beat was too strong,

the side of my face was all scratched up, my inner thighs and
calves streamed blood...

I entered a holy place in my mind, one devoid of all doubt
or fear.

Yet I did not for one second lose track in my mind of each moment's exact pressure needed to

maintain my angle. The wind was a hollow drone I simply thanked for drying my face.

Astonishingly enough, by not directly thinking about it, the ground below became more near.

As soon as my body learned the dance of the rhythm, I purposefully Forgot it so that I would

not adjust it. I became a dissimulation of myself climbing down a mountain, perhaps even

reading a poem, sipping lemonade, or watching television... Anything other than who and

where I was, since Death itself was possibly gunning for me. When my feet touched the

greensward I immediately knelt down and bowed and kissed the ground. My body was in

turmoil, my clothes all torn and stained in streaks of red. I thanked God and the Good Spirits

and enjoyed the luxury of a giggled laugh. This is what it's like to have fallen into love. /////
STANLEY GEMMELL /////// July 15, 2023

THE DAY YOU LIKED MY POEM

Cricket song near river's dragon-fly
Rows of shaking and slashed palms
Stately, glittering vessels afloat
upon the green and moving waters, oh,
Quiet and empty late of the cooled streets

Now that Fate is asleep
The royal offspring,
scion of the universe
flows through veins
both wild and steel-sured

So That:
Amid the crop cut symbols burnt into a meadow, like the
huge jet engines
Of A Risen Atlantis, whose use of no toxin to make massive
energy And
Who yawning whispers of gladdened hopes Smile secure And
Pats humanity on the head, the day you liked my poem

Full of beautiful coincidence, as if the mirror gave forth
Sacred Smoke,

As if the thousand handed deities exhibited Mirth,
And the places of dream began to suddenly Exist, oh,

Quiet and cool of the late dark's sleep, our city afloat in hope,
The manifold threads of the seasons guide wisest gathering
wise &

Stepping into the child-joy of fearless, unworried laughter:
I experienced the sliding of old things into the new:

Like Moonlight upon the solstice
At a circle of giant, ancient stones!

You are my calendar, Both
Feastdays and ordinary, You
Tell the time of my world!

Love makes of the unknown
That which is then shared.

(egos)
Merge in respectful gratitude,

Everyday always means this day;
And such gifts as Regard...
Precious When freely given; last through-out
And through; even every distance; the
Seeming separation.

My large, dark eyes (are) opening
The calf-stag's soul, my gaze of sweetnesses

Open themselves
Again and again

(while)

During dreams
For the one asleep (you or I)
The Other watches over...

_____

_____

STANLEY GEMMELL
July 15, 2023

If in a past life I had walked to your door, or you to mine, and failed to knock for the sweet

fear in one's heart, but soon there-after came Plague, or War, or some other sorrow

preventing either of us from approaching again, then this life not only serves our current

form, but likely, too, the past. We can imagine, just for the sweet Regard we currently

now enjoy for one another, that the fleeting whispers of hope that came to either

of our minds after the dissapointment of changed fate, have as their origin a

then-distant-future we currently engage. Oh sweet Spirit, so mysterious and pure,

that even after endless sorrow, comes an eternal cure, since, if now, once again, we two,

our love disrupted by life, we carry on regardless, eagerly awaiting the next chance.

The hollow forms we instead might have scorned, become lanterns and beacons to light

the way forward!

Stanley Gemmell
Micro-Glosse For Maria Talanova /////
July 15, 2023 #OfferedWithRespect #OfferedWithSincereLove

The man saw the image in the mirror
Move his mouth and then he heard
His own voice say:
"This is no longer Always.
Not business as usual,
But instead a rare pleasure.
It is vital that you know,
That you no longer break
The day's silence with
Mournful songs of secret love.
Remember the waves at your back.
Remember that the blush of her cheek
Is the sun."

———————————

———————————

NEITHER SELF NOR OTHER
Stanley Gemmell
July 15, 2023

The lichened dolmen, unhewn and dreaming, innocence itself, used to raise truth to heights
and to shield love from harm.. the dense citadel of packed hope, stone as old as time, moss
fresh grown with daybreak: as is a woman. Forever eternal limitless immortal Beauty undying,
unyielding. Fierce as the rain, gentle as the mud near to the springs.

S. Gemmell
DOLMEN FRAGMENT FOR MARIA
– July 18, 2023
Support her Boosty please at boosty.to/maria_talanovaaa

THE MORE THE WORLD HAPPENS
THE MORE I SAY YOUR NAME

poem by Stanley Gemmell
dedicated to Maria Talanova

A group of shaman astronomers
Attend to a poet's Song:

"My heart is in your hands
Your beautiful fingers cradle
And shelter my Other-World

(not against this one,
rather like an image,
not an actual place)

My soul is clay for you to mold
Since it serves truth

(Because Beauty is that which
may not be disavowed, nor
successfully slandered)

I spoke:
One day the world vented wrath
The next it wept, cooled by love

I spoke with nothingness
I held to soft angles

My every moment divined:
I became a vulnerable joy:

(The world avoids the anonymous
So a poet signs their name..)

(Friendships are a garden of trust
And poisoned by fears of flame)

(So as our sun burns too-hot
Our words repeated soothe and calm..)

A joy of hopeless love.
An open wound of sweetness-drenched hopes.

Oh, Thus:
Industry claims only sadness and sorrow
Are the mature world view, unless

You pay per episode, The machines
Of man are costly

(Even gardens became fruit fields,
Every being wanders)

But a painter, photographer or dancer
Finds joy from merest chance (no cost
To feel honored and special :-)

One day you will sigh
And if hope's fulfilled
be respected

Not for what you did or did not do
But for what you intended..

A more perfect symmetry.,
I have never found:
Your Senhal is Oltemat..

For you I shall write a created legend,
Out of the heaps and scraps of my life

& it won't matter how I am received:
an innocent among the carnage

I know deep down
I will have lived!"

After the fuschia comet
Filled the sky, briefly..

The learned men of the fields
Decided to name it and keep it..

Every two hundred and fifty
Times Twelve, or, Three Thousand
Cycles of years it is celebrated

The passing of a Great Age
Of human reckoning..

Such great love and joy
Shine from golden throated
Hopes Eternal
Such That
All are reminded of freedom
And virtue

_____
_____

July 18, 2023

THE HYPERCHARGE FRAGMENTS

Gold in naked fire: midday
White feathers in solitude: seagull
A slope of land bathes in breezes
Molecules dance in joy

The molecules are composed of atoms, the atoms composed
of fields
The first field holds on to itself
The second always reaches out to include
While the third is unknown, free and simple TO-BE

The neutronic field is your name
The emanation field is when it is said
The hypercharge field is when it is heard or used
like the letters to form a word
a word after another to make up sentences
and a collection of sentences to
make a paragraph or article
Oh, to roll your name across my tongue,
as it burns green-fuschia / A lazer of delight!

STANLEY GEMMELL

The rose that was found from Perul / Blushes more fiercely for its Shade /

Blood hued and drying its tears / The once polyswathed • in kisses /

Thought abandoned & derelict / Was shaping anew its miracle /

Soft against its stem / Silent to thorn / And bramble /

what once risen to itself / again and again / discovered /

measured & instantly exemplified / The rose that was found /

against sand and asphalt and heat / Drunk with hope /

like a wisened Lark Bird / Whose wing was stained by Dawn

—————————

—————————

"THE ROSE THAT WAS FOUND FROM PERUL..."
Stanley Gemmell
July 20, 2023
****

@maria_talanovaa
****

OH, WHAT NOBLE WORTH IS HE WHOSE LIFE

May see what he Loves!

I and my self boldly step into grave danger
At each and every solitary breath that I inhale
There exists the risk She for whom I live
Will not notice, that each Act I perform
Is in her Service,
(That)

The matters (of the Earth and Sea)
Little interest me unless it be for
Gaining further her Favor

And as for Sky and Space?
Much the Same!

I plead with the heavens
And command every hell
To do me this #Solid

If ever you see my eyes closed & at peace
Whether alive in this life or Next

If she still lives, then, to her speak my name
But if it be a growl or uncouth laff,
Then, instead, to Me So Say!

_____

_____

STANLEY GEMMELL
7/20/2023

How many days pass in just one hour?
How many lifetimes have I lived in this past week?
Everyday the sun cools a little bit,
But my raging joy becomes hotter,
I thank Goodness for all of it.

What I do may seem unusual.
I remain honest and I avoid being unkind.
The most important path for The Lover or Artist
Is as close as possible to the person or medium.

If you play a horn, understand that the Music is always on It;
If you love someone, know that it is for that One, that your
love exists.
Not the self, nor the others, is the music
Of the spheres ever played,
But instead it is for the delight of
The intelligence listening.

Oh, how beautiful and serene
It must be to grow and unfold
In hope and trust, in and among
A world of happy wildflowers!

The warriors and mages, savants
And audience of the universe
Pause - and then, move on.

KOLAPHOS (SPIRITUAL BLOW TO THE HEAD)
Stanley Gemmell
July 21, 2023

IF YOU WERE GONE ///// Oh my dearest Treasure / Oh my beam of white light /

The mere thought you have left / Fills my heart with dread / My soul has shaped its outline /

To reply to your silhouette / Every movement of your mouth / Is a poem found /

Upon a mountain / Your eyes are the swift flight / Of two eagles that dip shockingly /

In the blue sheet of air / Your arms are the two long bows / That myself an arrow must fly from /

Your face is the map of the earth and stars / Oh, if you were lost, / There would remain Nothing /

Neither breeze nor river / For me could flow / The objects would melt / Meaningless symbols /

Because meaning itself would Refuse! / The world would become sleep /

And happiness a mere rumor / Even if I laughed / There would be no sound /

So know that now / My spirit has forgotten what dreaming is for /

My lungs count every breath that I take / Because you are here and our world trembles /

Because you have not left: / This precious joy is Manifest! ///// ////////

Stanley Gemmell July 22, 2023

A is for Always B is for Better C is for Candid D is for Dance
E is for Ever F is for Friday G is for Goodness H is for Hope
I is for Interestimation J is for Jeweled K is for Karma L is for Lore
M is for Merman N is for Naked O is for Olfactory P is for Praise
Q is for Questing R is for Risen S is for Soulshook T is for Tops
U is for Ultimate V is for Vector W is for Woman X is for
Xylophone
Y is for Yes Z is for Zone

Thus, this is my Al-phable (or, All Fable, both are fine) and
what it means
Is that no matter the language or the letter, or the time, or
the clime
I always include you in my happy thought, and celebrate the
legends
And moments and miracles and fate, that brought us together,
And makes us both (happy and) smile.

_____

_____

ALPHABLE
Stanley Gemmell
July 22, 2023
In honor of Maria Talanova

** Note: There is no incorrect way to pronounce the title :-)
** And also, happy birthday to my honored Father, Mr. Gemmell who raised me and taught me and brought me up with respect!

THE POET ADDRESSES THE WORLD
ONE DAY AT AN HOUR AND PLACE
THAT MIGHT HAVE BEEN ANY OTHER
EXCEPT ONE OF HURT OR PAIN

"Seriously though, I am not even joking, you know I like you and I can only hope that you like

me back. You rise, you fall, you dawn, you set; all this is marvelous and I praise you, but.

I have to insist that you suddenly changed. Now, again, please hear me out, I don't mind

if you twitch, gesticulations, wild or not, definitely partake of the sacred, but you used to

be cool in the velvet, syrupy and purple places of my soul, crossing absentmindedly between

mundane thresholds of Rooms! Yes, I've fallen in love, but I am not from Lesbos,

where the greatest girl poet of all time, besides Enheduanna, lived... in other words,

you know me, I'm still the same person, and loving somebody has never prevented me

from honoring every previous love! To those who may have wished for me to fall in love

with them? I shall reveal a secret, no human controls it! Love is a living Transcendence

of all human will, that is why Romeo and Juliet should definitely have chilled out and waited, not gotten so crazy and dramatic, and that goes for any and all that feel the least bit slighted if

they wished for my attention and think they never got it! I am always a comment away.

But this is what I mean, World, you used to communicate clearly. There were no click-through

media lures, there were no chatbots or fakes. I always have been on the up and up and if

something I was exploring turned out to be wrong, I learned WHY and not only changed to

still partake of the status-quo, but preached the New or Recent Moral Message that I fortunately

got and never held back from fully incorporating it into everything that I do. World, you know

I have never been anything but a dedicated Student of Yours. I avoid killers, rapists, thieves

and sadists. I shun mind-games and time-wasting. When I make my sweet spiritual moments

and pictures, I stay humble and notice they manifest that way, also: humble and grateful; happy

just to help out -- of course, honored and hopeful for more, but always as sufficient to myself as

possible, so as to avoid forcing any thirst or hunger or craving or need unnecessarily onto any

other. What I DO appreciate about you is this: you always have paid me my due.

When folks or spirits greet me, you make sure they know it is really me that they deal with

and not some conglomerate or In-Part-Other. World, you have kept your Stanley, Stanley,

& made sure that others do so, as well. So, why the long face? Why suddenly temper-tantrum?

Do you blame me for others' faults, simply because you know that you CAN?

Aww, come on World, we both know you are Better than that. Anyway, I don't expect an

immediate answer (actually I would definitely prefer that you cool off a bit, especially if what you

intend to reply with is something that I will not like). Onto the second part of my reflection: a girl

I met and did not romance, earlier last night, a cool lesbian with prodigious powers of Gab (Gab means

Happy Babble,

or, light and fun conversation) turned on to me and, as usual, I noticed her words took on a more

serious edge the more that we exchanged them. I - always in defensive mode - did my best to

tone my expressions down, and sure enough, there was success. I was told to consider my

poetry as "Elaborations" ... Well. I had never, ever thought of that, and I certainly shall

consider it. But as a human being, and especially an internet enthusiast, I consider each

discrete communication act as fully parsed and independent of the last. I fell in love, World.

I fell in love like a bottomless well. I fell in love with Maria like a pit. But one made of a gigantic black sapphire with a black hole in the middle of it that sucks me into a white hole that is

invisible behind. So, now I am with her. And nobody else can enter, and either one of us may

leave at any time, and I certainly won't. And I try to keep it interesting enough that she will

not either. And I take it cool, calm and collected, casual and happy and day by day, because

I love her certainly, yes... but I also love love enough to know that the chances she will step

out for any reason, never preclude the chances she will want to come back in, after.

Life is long, but love is longer and I really and truly have nothing to lose, except the idea

and feeling "of it all" -- which definitely is not true, and I wish Romeos and Juliets around

the world to know this. If you love love enough to die for it, then you must know that love

feels much more honored when you choose to live for it, instead. Well, anyway, World...

My mom told me not to curse, otherwise you know I would tag you all up and hopefully

make you blush and feel radiant, exultant and all that great stuff... but I got to go.

You know I'm around, and I really hope to hear (good things) from you <3"

_____

_____

STANLEY GEMMELL
July 24, 2023

Infatuation, desire, support and admiration are like love:
they do not demand actions from the intended other,
they manifest energy FOR them and find something else
to do if they find out that it BOTHERS them, in any way.
:-) Cheers!

THE SUNLIT POEM

A girl on a slope
of hill
    All is
    green-angled

    Near the
    Smeared cleft of
Brook spilling quickly
Frothed and spuming waters

While all around whirls
As she whirls

    the ground

Like soft, brown
Soil drinks the rain

——

Had witnessed in a dream
A rough and still gleaming

Boulder of ruby
The size of her torso
Split into two pieces
One sheared like
Drizzled diamonds
And the other
As if it were
The rippled surface
Of a red-lit lake

And so, adventurously
Sought in search
For it

As the girl
Is in dream
So may the
Water bubble
and stream

———

For all
        Welcome

Love

None deny it,
Try as they may,

It is the e e r y
      n e g

            of creation

And heals & fathoms,
Saves and cures,
It is one thousand
Miles near infinity

And farther than
Any has ever gone

———

e e g
n r y
            oe
               From

         The   e
             earli st

———

"Certainly, you may not Yet
be able to praise her beauty
in her own language,
                    but look

how far you have already
                    come!"

"I know the words meaning
                    'I do not know,' & also
                    the greeting for
                                        'Good Morning!'"

"You see? You can already
get out of trouble by
protesting your ignorance;
as well as butter her up
in The Morning vya
                    Sweet Words!

My Son,
                    you are half-way There!"

———

Outside, sunbeams vye
with rain, your face
is in the leaves, with
your long, golden-brown
russet-tinged hair, I scry
the pale ivory of your cheek
touched by a white beam,
it slithers down your long
neck, soaked in melody,
drenched in hope, singing
an undying song, saying
it is time to live, the
water-droplets stream
along with it, in a happy,
shamanic dance to celebrate
the season, and for a moment,
I mistake my tears for them,
since I am dazed by good fortune
& all my love is mixed with dew!

———

You emerge Goddess
Of the DownPour

The sweetness of your
round curved mouth

& the pinkness of your lips
Fascinates

So from the side of your glance
I know see five green Kimodos

Elegant and Sage with
Quick movements to full-stop

You pull upon the taut cords
Of the clouds above

To draw down electric
Grey-Blue Lightening Rays!

———

The Green-Wood Stirs
The leaves come Alive

A shir of the wind
With the sound of birds

Moves like the force
of their wings

Love is like this:
Unexpected and cool

And exalted and invisible
And revered

It is a jewel of twelve facets:
One for each Moon of the year

In which you dwell
En-Sceptred by The Good!

———

All the stars reveal themselves
The sun and the rain
Now yield themselves
To Night
                    But in your eyes
                    You carry the sun
                    Still: in your look

Dream and wood now mix
Together with the brood
Of flying and crawling
And soft padding Things
That we have termed
As life: but, I still hear
The silent song of hope
All the while

     That you dance
     To the quiet of the Moon!

———

"Did you learn anything
    new? Tell me."

"I learned how to say,
    'OK. I know, I love you.'"

"This is good. How does
    it feel to say?"

"Actually different. And
    better than anything I
    will ever say."

"Because you found words
            whose sound will only ever
            be meant for one person."

"Yes."

"OK. I know, I love you."

"Agreed."

———

Sunlight at night is
curious.

A hazy remnant and also
promise

Photons pass through solid
objects.

Yes, but, of sunlight there
is never doubt:
            even the
            smallest amount
                still counts.

Sunlight at night is curious
because darkness itself
is lit:

               people insist what
      small bright there is, is!

———

Morning time,
the sun returns,
was sleep in dream
or has dream become Form?

The radiance dazzles
We are beside a pool :
You and I linger :
Become lovers born !

As we stare in each
                other's eyes

Our mouths part
               to open

And intone one
        Sacred Word:

Ah-bw-oo-n . . .

———

The absolute, darkness &
            light in One

        Radiance

Birthing, Flowing, Giving

        Forth

The breath & the Spirit

           `*pneuma*

The vibration of Love

        Interpenetrates

        Form!

—

A girl on a slope by a pool
Her body is dazzling,
Curved and sleek,
Her breathing quickens,
Her smile shapes
The landscape within,
Her arm reaches out
To touch my body
My eyes involuntary:
Close

Existence-At-Pause

My blood chills then boils
Then, again, froths !

Delight of all things
The soft skin of her face
Touches mine . . .

—

As I lower my face to hers
I remove all uncertainty

And like a magnet
That is drawn

As I reach around her torso
To draw her close to mine
There is a new form made
Like a mountain makes
A spring

Hatha-Ya
        A name
        An action
        A sign
        A thing

Made from I and Yes
Made from the seat
        of Queen & King

The sound itself a *magique*

———

In the magic
Of a purple embrace
All things begin to ponder

Red carnation drinks
her own sweat

Clouds turn to sugar
and dissolve
                then reform
as your teeth
                Awen bit
                my lips and my own

Mud sparkles
Mixes with gold
That boils
All troubles
Down to their looks

Oh, Harmony,
happily fade with us
deeper into yourself!

——

Gray matter
Gentle wind
off stars,
Chants Thusly :

I, Awen, have
Discoursed greatly upon
Hatha-Ya, the sibilant Mystery,
Holy Dracun Green & Pink,
Most Discrete & Complete Bliss,

But, I have a New Series
of Dates & Details,
concerning She,
for you now:

Upon the third day
of high Smmer's
Waning Moon -->

Give her her Freedom
Let her go . . .

———

The first detail is
Again, to the sun,
And its pleasance,
May it shine, bright

But cool, enamored
Of Earthly Restraint

&

While the second is
The moon, and its
Shock and grandeur
Unto Venus . . .

May you Live
With All-Good
Memory

May you forever
Achieve your
Every Quest

———

And simply and suddenly
Love
                    Welcomed All

The flood gates were opened
The birds & beasts sang &
Cried in Empery

The search for it
Was it being

 Found !

———————————

———————————

Stanley Gemmell
AUGUST 4, 2023

PUKING WITH JOY I FEEL LIKE MY HEAD IS FILLED WITH CRAZY HOPE I THINK TO BE WORTHY TO BY YOU AM LOVED IT MAKES ME MORE SANE I THINK EACH TIME

to get to that thought It can be hard
and palpable Your excellence is paramount

my self as felt slippery, I have often
others Something can see, not but me

Then happened, YOU in the same way
As every other place, people or thing
that was... ever

                with but one important
                :différance

You stayed you and chose me.
of Out the chaos hardship, and
its or opposite else, a perfected
Elegance of Fate you that always,
Already, in this life, enjoyed,
me before

and that somehow I thought I would
or even somehow thought Could I that
drain ruin or Possibly
you then And smiled
And this Rain became

nourishment The I did not realize I needed
than More any other.

strengthened Now and healed,
I speak out purposeful against
deception

I champion
The fearless beauty and hope
Of honest offered-love, again
(Safe to exist, happy to breathe
Free from entrapments or snares)

Like a newborn Colt in covered
and Moisture breath, trembling and
Because it knows how free and fast
It will someday run:

Lovers born to Hope selfless
And Wisdom smile as they weep
And shine like the sun!

_____

_____

Stanley Gemmell
7/24/2023

I FEEL LIKE PUKING WITH JOY MY HEAD IS FILLED WITH CRAZY HOPE TO THINK I AM WORTHY TO BE LOVED BY YOU MAKES ME MORE SANE EACH TIME I THINK IT

It can be hard to get to that thought
Your excellence is paramount and palpable

I have often felt my self as slippery,
Something others can see, but not me

Then YOU happened, in the same way
As every other people, place or thing
that ever was...

                but with one important
                difference:

You stayed and you chose me.
Out of the chaos and hardship,
Or else its opposite, a perfected
Elegance of Fate that you always,
Already, in this life, enjoyed,
before me

and that I thought I would somehow
or even thought that I somehow Could
Possibly ruin or drain

        And then you smiled
        And this became Rain

The nourishment I did not realize I needed
More than any other.

Now strengthened and healed,
I speak out against purposeful
deception

I champion
The fearless hope and beauty
Of honest love-offered, again
(Safe to exist, happy to breathe
Free from entrapments or snares)

Like a newborn Colt covered in
Moisture and breath, and trembling
Because it knows how fast and free
It will someday run:

Lovers born to selfless Hope
And Wisdom smile as they weep
And shine like the sun!

_____

_____

Stanley Gemmell
7/22/2023

POEM OF THE THIRD PERSON

///// He was exalted before he was born, in the uncreated space
that she was yet to occupy. His mother was the Earth that mixed the waters with the stars of
the sky. His father was light, shine of ceaseless travel & infinite renown. All the place of
dreams existed, for him, in the body of the woman who taught him Love. The Lady was not
ordinary, although she appeared like everyone else, to walk upon two graceful legs, with feet
of living tigers. Her back was a great river, her spine of alabaster, fine-grained gypsum, the
mineral deposits shone. Her hips two massive pillars, like the hundred-fifty foot (or, 50 meter)
tall white basalt vary-structured towers of Russia's Cape Stolbchatiy. Her chest was the massive
steppe, whose rugged torso bore infinite marks, of glorious and fateful struggle amongst the
winds and snows and rains. Her shoulders were the two domes of a golden and round
observatory, which studied the movements of all of life of a Universe which sometimes
preferred to shrug. One day, she taught him a fable... about two of four points which fascinated

and intrigued him. She said, "My love. Do you not know that when I weep each of my eye

follows its own axis? I will tell you about my Left eye, which has fathomed the glorious colors

and moods of those things near to us. The many rooms and windows and views, which are

obtained and granted to us. The brilliant hues and bright-dabbed speckles upon the fantastic

birds who near us in song. The lively sounds and anecdotes from the cosmic seas that stream

along those various paths. One is a great and darkly massive hidden. A mystery one may solve,

if only for the sweet satisfaction of answering the riddle of why what nears and when. It is a

crisp and black, oily well, with shaggy neon blues, that fringe and quake and grasp and stretch

into fibers and tendrils of white light, and then darkens again, AND again, again is lit. The other

is the hottest thing to near us, although it is eight-thousand-four-hundred-and-eighty light years

away! It burns at three-hundred-and-seventy-seven-thousand-five-hundred-and-forty degrees

Fahrenheit (or, 209,726 degrees Celsius) degrees! It had slipped off its dress of Hydrogen and

made those near it, fall to their knees! I tell you this, my One who is Mine, because my Left eye may witness to the simple truth that from where we stand, these two objects form a straight

line." He felt the shudder of her sweet words. The cadence of her mouth, in concert with the

music of her Love. She moved her face so that her profile stood, for a moment, clear as a

sweet, glaciered and melting cliff-face... whose waters weaved a series of wells with curiously

ambered honies. At night he dipped his hands into her tears to taste if they were sorrowed, or

joyed. What difference could it make to a man who felt as if the fountain were ever-born? He

could feel her smile as he closed his eyes, and wept himself with a slow and easy shrug. /////
/////// Stanley Gemmell, July 25, 2023

GRALE

1

This is one of the many fables taught by a sunbeam to a yellow-topaz mermaid, fiery-lily, water-tiger girl who sometimes grew purple and fuschia faerie wings from her back to fly out from the pool she liked best to live inside, at night, often at New Moon -when it were most private ...

"Hello, Dear One, and I very much hope you like this story. It is, most definitely, partly true, as all the great fables are, however, many of the morals most people seek in such animal-confabulations are not quite apparent, or most usually expected, therefore, do not be surprised if it were misinterpreted, accidentally, as actual fact, instead of symbolic myth... Enjoy!"

Before mankind grew numerous upon Earth, and while Angels were still only dimly aware of their responsibility to the new species called Human, there was a stark and beautiful Hill near a meadow-land.

Upon this hill, which was russet-color, a dark red made from the gathered collection of many crashing sunsets, was a large Dolmen, or, boulder which had green moss growing upon it.

In the primeval dawn of our Aeon, the separation between mineral, vegetable and animal kingdoms was less discrete. Many stones and gems took upon themselves sometimes frightful souls.

It happened that Yellow Topaz had great responsibility, then. Diamond was derelict, basking in the composted awe of its massivities of pressure. Sapphire often took the lead in the direction of Force.

It was not known exactly when, many whispered that it had happened upon the very First Day of Creation. That an awful Ruckus was heard from the heavens.

The stones took upon themselves a Querie and sent forth to fetch a Crome Beast: so named for its utter frugality in eating. It had the body of a slick, green and golden-light streaked and glittering dolphin, with the wings and talons and beak and eyes of an eagle, and some had dolphin snouts and some had eagle's beaks, depending upon their sex and occupation.

The Crome that had appeared for the summons had a fiery red hued eagles beak and scintillating, sky blue eyes. Its skin was very green and though it were a fierceom warrior, it were femenine and female, just the same. She reported from the nearby, Northern Seas, and this being while still our world was very young, the white-glittered ice fell from her

wings that she bate. The strokes of each beat causing massive
fluctuations in wind and space, although the creature was
not large, so potent were its strokes. She received glittered
and random quartz bits from which to choose her morsel, or,
crumb, and depending on whether she ate or not, this was,
in itself, seen as an augury.

2

The emerald fell from Lucifer's crown
On the first day of Creation
When beautiful as he was
He failed the Test of remaining humble

The green thing fell to Earth and burned in the Atmosphere
So that its tint even loosened from its form
Just enough so that when it splashed in the sea
It lent the area an eerie green luminensce

The strange object was eaten and then freed
When the creature died or itself was eaten

It was prodded nudged pulled and played with
It was attacked and worshipped, avoided and sought for

In various ways across the many planetary Ages
Until at the time when Jesus walked with Woman and Man

It was brought to him as a gift
The Master knew it for what it was
But he did not say a thing
Instead he performed a healing

The green stone had suffered every day that ever existed
Because of the use it had first been put toward...
Our Lord God (whether you agree or not, it matter{s} little
since Christ himself says, 'If they do not believe, brush
the sand off your sandals and simply walk on, Peace
Be unto All...' -- therefore, don't think The Poet
is pushing religion, I'm not, I'm telling a Story) then
Raised it aloft and held The Last Supper and used It
As the Chalice, to hold the wine which in later Truth
Became his Blood, during the Sacrificial Rite of The Eucharist

Again the Emerald was lost. While Jesus was flayed and
mortified,
Joseph of Arimathea held onto it and collected sacred drops of
Our Savior's Blood into it, and thus from Infamy Itself,
Was born the Holy Grale

ARION

The greatest poet in the world / survived kidnapping in this way: / the bandits who had robbed him / asked him to sing just before they / forced him to jump into the sea. / They did not know / that, nearby, many dolphins were listening. / These dolphins were sorrowed / and outraged that such a fine talent / was being put to death. / They swam to him after the villains / on the boat, after mocking / and gloating, had / turned their backs. / Arion was fully clothed, / they laughed and chittered / and prodded him with their snouts. / The dolphin spun and also sang / and the poet and the creatures / turned the ocean into a happy shout! // The villains arrived at Arion's city. / "Your master has been lost / at sea," they lied... / with greed in their eyes / thinking of all the riches / they had promised to transport / but actually had stolen. / The mayor-king was sorely grieved: / How can this be? / He thought. / Our greatest treasure is now Gone. / The entire city wept. / The bandits were amazed. / The chief among them wished to suddenly leave. / The mayor-king gave them leave to go / and thanked them for bringing / this important news & then explained / that it was very hard to harbor and home Arion. / His beauty and majesty made some go insane / for all sorts of different reasons / mainly because there was no explanation / for it. / Another difficulty, the mayor-king continued / was the yearning! / All the citizens hounded him. / Over the years they had gotten better / at not immediately gushing a Request, / but instead to control themselves / and let him walk by, in peace. / The citizens took pride in this, / and remembered to be kind / to the many tourists who / visited, hoping to hear Arion sing. // At the awareness of / the sorrow Arion's death will have caused, / the mayor-king's head lowered, / and their eyes filled with tears / that gushed and fell and splattered / the dust on the ground / next to their feet. / When, suddenly, dripping wet / tired and bedraggled / And quite upset by the ordeal, / Arion appeared.

//

The leader of the bandit pack drew his sword / the other villains had left theirs upon the boat. / No words were exchanged, / there was no need to explain. / The citizens were more hurt / than shocked. They thought / 'We have suffered / the cruelest lie ever told.' / The best and most loved among them / quickly took the poet by the arm / silenced his protest with a finger over their mouths / shook their heads quickly while staring at the ground / as they ushered him away / with rapid, measured footsteps. // Years later, Arion traded his gold / and rare and fine objects / in exchange for land. / People came from near and far / to possess an item / that once was his! / The greatest wonder in all the world / (to them) was how his songs / always

111

improved. It was / downright Mystical. Anyway, of course, / Arion was wildly successful, / and late in his life / he delighted in the responsibility. / To make sure his boarders and renters were / comfortable and happy, / he built the finest homes, with / the richest views. / He forgave late payment / and held special feasts to honor good neighbors. / He forced truth from others / by accident of his own truth.

///

Years passed and those who grieved / the bandits were forgotten. / They simmered in dangerous and wild / unknown lands. / They created a curious prayer: / the opposite of memory and song / they even forced each other to forget their own names. / They did this to hurt even the idea of Arion's grace. / It was the only way / they could convince themselves / that they had actually won, and not Him. / Eventually, since their numbers grew numerous / and the many lands they traversed / adopted this blight and error: / to be against memory and honor / (and Truth) just to think or feel themselves / more free. / Arion's lands became forgotten, too. / His songs were not preserved. / His memory faded to a rumor. / Except the creatures, themselves. / Birds and dolphins and mice and lizards / all still love him. / This is why their law is Hospitality / and each take care / to honor the other's Sensibility. / Turtles and snails are the most revered, because, like sloths / they love Arion's songs the most. ///// /////// Stanley Gemmell * July 24, 2023

MOSCOW LOCAL TIME AS FELT FROM FLORIDA

AT 3:09 AM I found out how fragile you are.
The strange fact remains, you are strong
So most will not consider your vulnerability.

AT 3:10 AM you will have not known for
Certain that I began to compose this poem:
If I include it in our book it will be part of the third

Section. The first describing the thrill.
The second describing the mystery.
The third describing the limits.

So. I will continue to compose
& also to suppose that
Knowledge that limits

Is also quite useful! I will give
An example: suppose we became
So happy that it angered the world

(without our knowing) and simply

Continued on, As-Is. Until one fateful
Day the world achieved a Vengeance

And separated one or the other
From an important dream.
The dream being something

Easily achieved had we noticed
Joy as something not belonging
To the joyful, but instead as a loan.

Well. I, myself, always pay my debts.
I keep my word and notice that you
Are even better at such dependability.

Perhaps this poem will demonstrate
To you that you deserve protection:
Being vulnerable is also a call to safety.

I would happily satisfy you
Before the urge to lose faith
Ever became an action.

I choose All, upon this special
Holiday, because Nothing
Has nothing to do with Love.

———————————

———————————

Stanley Gemmell - July 26, 2023

We were alone and together with Night
Night gave us Moon Moon gave us Thought
Thought gave us Love Love gave us Hope
My She says to me, "Tell me a Truth? Please?"
I said, "Of course," and smiled.

"I do know what Everything is.
It is the decision on what and how
to limit Anything." She shook her head Naw.

I nodded and prodded her belly gently,
Making her smile, My She still lost in Thought
Said, "Because that is still artificial, you are not
Accounting for things, you are only referencing
The mechanism For things. I know I'm right,
On this one, you finally Lose! Haha!"

She beamed happily and immersed herself in the various
Idea of the particularates which compose our world.
Thinking, No stinking limit accounts for Anything, at all!
I continued, "Listen, you are paying attention to every
Thing except the Decision itself. Without the choice
[to call a halt to the next thought and state, here, at last
is Everything]
Anything still exists, but there can never be a chance for

Everything. [Because Anything would be the next Thought
to follow the success of the manifested Everything,
Something must always happen after Something
happens]" Undaunted, she replied, "So what,
Just because you may or may not, or are able to
Or not able to, Encompass [Whatever], does not render
[Thusly] Existence [As, or, to be] either contingent [dependent]
or immanent [completely and unstoppably realized,
or in the process of full realization].
Plus, the limit happens to be more
Important than the decision, [even though
you tried to place the decision in service
of its limit, the decision actually exists,
and does something, while the limit
only modifies]
Because it may exist independently of it,
Yet a decision cannot Be unless there is
Included in the very grounds of its presence, Yes,
The limit." I had kissed her shoulder, gently.
Her eyelashes startled me, she had the ability
To see from the corner of her eyes.
"You are a Total Angle Master, ok, but,
we speak of Everything. Obviously you are
Of the persuasion that a definition for a pronoun
Details every instance of its usage. [that the word
He refers to every he that ever was, is and will-be]

The everything

From four years ago at an earlier hour, compared

To how this everything evolved after an incident,

And then each time this word is used, in an ideal

World and Mind, every possible variation of its Truth

Is actually rendered. You are cosmic."

She nodded, perhaps. She was able to nod without moving.

I certainly felt as if she had nodded.

"Agreed, and why should this present a problem?

Why should a possibility such as the correct usage of a totality

Necessarily be impossible for a human usage, especially when

sincere.

You are my everything. Should I then persuade you to limit

The meaning of this usage?" I was not giving up. I asked

My Her gently, "If I decide that Everything is the limit,

But then consider a Revelation to have always, already

Been included in such Everything, was I in error before

That which is Greater revealed itself to me? No, correct?

Therefore, any usage of the word signifying Totality

Can be ---" She finished my sentence and rolled

Her eyes, truly her beauty was shocking, "Provisional."

"Yes, exactly, I claim that the only handle upon the ---"

She did it again except even more beautiful, "Possibility."

"Yes, the Possibility of a correct rendering for the usage,

'Everything' must be when you decide to do it." Her eyes

Flared wondrously, like skies or oceans or night itself

Were volcanoes. "You are wrong. Everything exists,
And it is made up of many discrete instances of
Something, that are able to be added up and
Counted altogether, even thoughts. Plus, I
Consider there to be sentient beings able to know it.
They need not make any decision to know it, partial
Or complete and you are exhibiting mere human vanity
To suppose that by hiding your head in metaphyical sand
The wind cannot ever storm. This is a very human Avenue
You have brought me down." I felt extremely guilty
Because I could not remove my smile. Her shining person
Was as if a magnet planet found the two metal bits
I called my eyeballs. I just closed my lids over them.
I was in the hope for shame, but just felt like crying
Tears of joy, instead. No epithet could be found
For either her grace, or my astonishing good luck
At being so near to it.

———————

———————

ACCIDENTAL HYPNOSIS
Stanley Gemmell
July 27, 2023

GIRL AS SWAN

The four steps of the swan had
Become automatic
The first was to re-name
The second was to re-mean
The third was to re-aim
The fourth was to re-deem
The four steps of the swan had
Made way for the fifth
The fifth step was to rejoice...
The girl as swan told me these things
Not to be anything but nice, she
Did it with a beautiful shrug
And cautioned fruitfulness
And expansion of love
She said, "No matter what."
I stared at her lovely neck.
I wept with no tears, but
Instead my spirit flewed.
I knew what she meant.
That even swans should
Flee the impure, if
They are mid-flight,

Doing fifty-five,
From Boston to New York,
And happen to glance down
At the wrong time...
"Bah, same thing as St. Pete
To Moscow, something about
A beautiful thing traveling
South, recalls the concept
named 'Fiasco,' yet, never
you mind, Milieu, you will see
it will have been worth it,
to see the monuments,
to propitiate the symbols
of hopeful joy and raging peace,
once again. Trust me, it is worth it."
The girl or swan, might have said . . .

STANLEY GEMMELL
JULY 28, 2023

** fifty-five is a reference to the American National Speed
Limit of fifty-five miles per hour, which was in effect for
many, many years (now it varies) and is the swan's top-
speed of flight. St. Pete references St. Petersburg, Russia,

not St. Petersburg, Florida (although they are related: St. Petersburg, Florida's history dates back hundreds of years, it's Russia connection - by name - began in 1888. Legend has it, co-founders John Williams of Detroit and Peter Demens [originally Pyotr Dementyev] of St. Petersburg, Russia made a bet on who got to name the city.)

THE SACRIFICE ///// /////// People think I'm crazy because I take a chance and fly away somewhen you are always here glinting green in the fallen sands of a new beginning all day is the same everyday I had thought about since 1978 eight thousand seven hundred and ninety one times per second How to explain it kissing my pillow crying bitter tears of raging feasts of joy growing into the presentiment and passing people like roadsigns blessing everyone either or always rising above planting seeds in the miracle of hope yes once before I never ever got the hang of asking why thanks to oceans inside Can I ever raise my eyes laughing so ridiculously my eyes burning green and blissful tears slow shaking friendship of lightning and sugar Oh white glazed and powdered milk of happiness The stern and serious play of arrival could always skip a heartbeat and still make it home Sunlight glints off the gathered waves All the gods have spoken The Christ in perfect harmony grants them the air upon which Their soundwaves roam With nothing more than the perfect hands of a girl More beautiful than facets More perfect than the roaming center of the circle Slow horned honies of viscous warmth and joy Holy musk of the late AM ///// /////// *STANLEY GEMMELL July 29, 2023*

THE DAY YOU SAID GOOD MORNING

Like a stairway into the stars
The blonding white fires of hope
Leading me forwards and up
A cloud serves as a pillow
A rainbow made into a teacup
An army of unicorns
With golden, spiral horns

A fabulous vista
Of every glory crowned
A magnificent array
Of girlhood, like the
Rising tide . . .
I planted a tiny galaxy
Into the salted surf's sand
I held my ear to the ground

While the ivoried foam
Played across my face

I heard the sweet sighs
Of love insane with joy

I felt the flame that
Did not burn
I moaned and slowed
My haste
I wept with joy
Into the sea
Only you, could I taste!

Good morning
Good morning
And a third song
Good morning
Birds became trumpets
Dolphins surfed the waves
Spinning smooth and green
As the spiral-horned horses
Rushed the shore!

As sweet Providence
Provides your voice
Tah-Tah, and again Tah!
No wonder I am vibrant
Since you made fruit
Of what was once the sun!

Let us eat now,
Let us partake,
Soon it will be dark
And I have no knowledge
Of if again I will wake!
But I promise to hope
Without ceasing:
To hear such Blessing
From your lips, Again!

—————————————

—————————————

STANLEY GEMMELL
July 29, 2023

LOVE POEM

Immortal life resides in your eyes
Your slanted cheekbones rain

The slope of forehead a pale crown
Against all idolatries

You sit and mix with the salted wind
Near the Northern Seas

Your woman's lips shudder & slip
Between the infinite dimensions

Oh drumbeat of woman
Your proud and high breast
is as young as the ocean

And fallen into dream
And every wild quest

Your fantastic heartbeats

Oh eyelids of the planets
Saturn & Pluto

>   yet warm

>   as Sol are you

Forever bequeathed forever to me
To know enough, at least, to love you

Let zero blame
And even less cost

Let Myrhh sticky sweet
To Wander!

>   Let Boast

>   Aggravate

Let most lose Focus!
For here we have

>   Woman & Love

>   At The Eternal Locus!

I love you for who you are
I love you for what you're not
I love you and serve you
and Adore

>   with every fiber

of my being
every second I'm alive
The honied tears drip from
Your eyes, Oh Goddess & Rain
Oh, Heaven free from Pain,
Although you suffer
you are redeemed
with the hopeful kisses
of the summer's unexpected Joy

I love you forever
And each moment more
To lose you is to die
Before I am born

I love you for the sound
You make to scatter all sorrow!

Thank you for my life
Because it was unknown
Until you scattered
The white pearls
Of earthly wisdom
Among the white stars

Your long arm reached up
And I suddenly knew
I was breathing

Life is precious now
And bliss is fragile
But Eternal!

—————————————
—————————————

STANLEY GEMMELL
July 31, 2023

APPENDIX

Selective Mnemopsychosis
(Literary Theory, 2000-2023)

Here is a Chaos of poetic response. I will also keep to an ethical theory describing "Care", "Sorge", "Dread", or primordial concern, primitive self-mandated hyper-vigilance as it relates to the Other, any other. This translates to a responsibility I have toward my fellow beings, whose unshielded face is exposed to death continually. I have a duty (even before the idea of duty may be fully known, recognized, or mediated) to the face of my fellow sufferer (suffering risk, loss, chance, love, laughter, fear and victory) even before I can properly identify or define a duty to my 'self'... as it is the very being of the Other which grants me my self, via contrasting differance.

I will be specifically and more or less rigorously concerned with temporality as it enframes this project. Not just time, specifically, will be of essence in my critical response, but specifically, the "Instant". That impossible fiction of time, in time, and thru time which perhaps orders a certain human sensibility, a certain human pathos, concerned as it is with an at once fictional-yet-functional moment. Quantum mechanics explains how life and its so-called particulars, its particles, should be viewed as wave-forms. In other words, there is no such a thing, scientifically, as "the instant", yet this concept is made much use of by the citizens of the world. And finally, as relates to the fundamental nature and quality, question or reality of "ontology" the study of Being, the aesthetic ethic. The physical, sensory, moral aptitude of reader/ writer/ artist/ art form.

There is the transcendental harbor, sanctuary, asylum or protectorate of temporality. There is the negative energy of the infinite phase (and this leads to a negative theology, or an approximation of Gd as a reflexion of Gd's absence). And finally there is the ultimate Cause or origin of causality (which may or may not be a fiction).

Therefore, in no particular order, and with no stratified agenda, I present to you these Anergic Micro Reviews. Perhaps the first installment in a series, and less concerned with the books or media themselves, than with the event of their unfolding.

SELECTIVE MNEMOPSYCHOSIS
stanley gemmell

Memory can be said to be institutive of reality. Inaugurating reality by means of proxy. Memory is apprehended by the mnemonic apparatus. So named from Mnemosyne, the Greek goddess of memory and mother of the Muses. Mnasthai, to remember, is what gives birth to Grace.

The past exists insofar as it can be siezed inside a structure of space. The universe can be defined in terms of a three dimensional grid. The universe is not infinite (since it is expanding), however it is not practical to designate a current mathematical value as such.

The universe is made up of matrix sized points of reference which form the three dimensional grid. Each individual matrix point has its own individual reference signature.

The universal grid is the framework of the universe whose purpose supports the environment we know as existence. Everything in existence contains part of this grid. The grid is fixed in relation with the universe, it does not move, however all that exists within this grid can. These grid points are not imaginary reference points (otherwise we would exist in a void). The existence of this grid allows things to have shape, size, quality and quantity, etc. Since everything moves on this grid, then everything has the same basis, the same origin, the same common denominator.

The grid is the combination of all the base matrix delta origin points. All the base matrix delta origin points are spaced equally throughout the universe. The base matrix which emanates from its delta origin point is fixed in reference to the position in the universe. The base matrix delta origin points are the universal grid.

Space should be viewed as a lattice with a base uniform delta structure. A delta structure is the individual construction of a bar in a matrix structure. A matrix is the pattern of a matrix structure. A matrix structure is a single complete structure consisting of fields.

An atom consists of fields being the neutronic field, the unified charge field and the emanation field. The neutronic field is a field constituting the boundary of an object where its value is the result of (1+1=1). The unified charge field is the concept replacing the concept of an electron as a charged particle. This unified charge field is neither negative nor positive but unified, it has no opposite. It attracts to other unified fields, but also to the neutronic field.

The attraction of the unified charge to the neutronic field is greater than the attraction of the unified charge to another unified charge, therefore the concept of (1+1=1) applies to unified charges. Neutronic field is not attracted to a neutronic field. Think of water droplets. They merge but remain singular. Thus is how the concept of (1+1=1) works.

All this is the effect of the emanation field. The emanation field is the atom and emanates from a center point. An emanation field is not attracted to another emanation field and remains neutral. The emanation of the atom is in constant motion, this motion could be described as the forming of individual points, where each individual point is formed one point at a time with such speed as to appear as a complete emanation.

These individual points are emanation fields, the boundaries of the emanation fields form the single neutronic field surrounding the number of atoms in a unit(y). The atoms must be compatible, capable of meshing together if they are to form a neutronic field (for example, in chemistry, some atoms won't bond), then they must be allowed to get close enough together to be able to mesh (this process includes many variables). The close meshing of the atoms is part of what forms the structure of the universe, meaning every single atom is in close proximity to the next.

The unified charge produces the emanation field (the atom), the emanation fields rub and create basic energy by hypercharging.

The emanation is not the only part of the atom which is in motion as the unified charge is also in motion. The unified charge field is attracted to other unified charge fields, and to emanation fields, but the attraction of the unified charge to the emanation field is greater than its attraction to other unified charges. The emanation is the source of the neutronic field because the neutronic field exists at the boundary of the emanation field, of the emanation fields when they mesh.

The One ("1"), the neutronic field, exists as a result of, finds its source in, or equals ("=") the ever moving, always blurring edges of each emanation field [in the already internally separate(d)compound of One plus One ("1+1")]. Thus, 1+1=1 is always, already totally differentiated within itself while paradoxically remaining unified, singular and identical to itself. Thus it is identical to itself and different to itself and within itself. It is also woven into the very fabric of our existence, comprising, at the very least, the physical material of our astral plane, if not also the spiritual.

The effect of the unified charge in relation to the emanation field is called basic hypercharging. Hyperhcharging increases the unfied charge level of the object beyond its natural charge level which in turn effects the emanation field which grows larger (gets stronger) due to the increased level of unified charge which could be described as fuel for the emanation field.

When the emanation field gets larger it has an increased interaction with the matrix structures beside it which are also doing the same thing. This extra interaction would be considered as a change to the natural vibration of the matrix. While matrix structures are in their natural state their emanation fields interact with an action that could be described as a rubbing.

This rubbing has the effect of producing the unified charge. The natural action of matrix structures produce unified charges. So one of the effects of hypercharging an object is an increase in the size of the object due to the emanation field growing larger (getting stronger)
which is the effect of the changed unified charge. This also happens with regard to weight due to the unified charge attracting to other unified charges, making an object which then contains more unified charge.

Hypercharging dilates the neutronic field. It weakens (1+1=1) at the point of 1+1 due to the emanation fields getting larger and pushing away from each other. Each 1 in 1+1, remember, is an emanation field. This effect could be considered as a change in density. The effect of dilating the neutronic field in an object such as a waterdrop allows that object to be added to. The dilated state could be considered the melting point. Total dilation is the separation of 1+1. Basic energy derives from the rotational action of this dilation. The atoms of the universe melt freely

138

into each other, hypercharging each other's existence into sequential change which occurs within a fixed grid of structures.

This grid can be seen as a result of a gripping consciousness. There are certain objects (particles so small) which only come into existence from our study of them. They are necessarily altered and changed permanently from our attention. Our attention fixes them into existence and, since they only came into existence from our attention (because our attention had already altered them, or changed them, thus forcing them to constitute a new state, thus effecting that state, their state, their new state).

These fields of attention create emanation fields. An emanation field consists of a fixed structure that emanates from a fixed center point. The design on which the universe is based may be called the base matrix. This common origin or basis is the universal grid itself. No matter what the object is, it is made from the same base matrix design as the next object with the difference being its internal delta and sub delta field values. Remember that the delta structure is the individual construction of a bar in a matrix structure (in this case, the universal matrix). A sub delta is a delta structure whose delta origin point is different from the main delta origin point. The sub delta level is a reference made to the number of
sub delta levels in a matrix structure.

The law of Cup-Cup is a function in relation to the universal grid. When objects move around on the grid they do so using what is called the law of Cup-Cup. This law governs the actions of possibility in reference to their ratio values, which henceforth determine the possibility of that action. A ratio is a mathematical combination used for calculation and description of structure.

When we remember, we activate fields. The definition of a field is not something that can be defined in terms of one thing or another. The interaction of fields should never be viewed in terms of attraction and repulsion since this concept is dependent on the existence of opposites which can not be proven. A field is a point of reference in relation to the reference of that point whereas the values of all points are taken into consideration. This means that a field is not only an interaction value at a specific point of reference. So a field is also merely an effect as is the whole universe. It is the value of a field that determines what word or description gets applied to that condition for the purpose of communicating any such event.

Our memory field is such that no negative thing or value may authentically exist within it. Since what is comprised by our memory field (even if it be unremembered) includes all of the past, present and future. It includes the past and future (which are never fully present) by indicating where the presence of all that is present diverges from both past and future. By expressing what has already happened, memory manifests what is happening and therefore affects and effects what will happen.

The memory field is made selective to the degree that one decides whether its contents point towards the past or to the future. Each conscious selection of orientation, each decision as to whether something in the memory field points to something that did happen or could happen, remarks intentionality.

Value as such may be expressed as a possibility within a conscious event-space.

To be responsible to or be responsible for such possibility, value, may be to participate in a series of call-and-answer structures. Since the articulation of responsibility points firstly to the 'xistence of An Other, and secondly to the availability of The Other as a communicant.

This responsibility circumscribes Chaos within a regime of Difference. Chaos is made to be precisely that which stands outside of any decision to stand for something.

This is to say that Chaos becomes the neutronic field in which the emanations of our decisions to uphold certain values melt and cause each other upheaval, ultimately devoured.

The memory field finds its origin and fundamental end in Chaos, yet articulates radical separation from and difference to Chaos. Music admirably articulates this simultaneous acceptance of and rejection of Chaos. This use of Chaos to go beyond Chaos and this beyond of Chaos making use of Chaos as its fundament.

The artistic image (be it visual, sonic or other-sensory) expresses the origin of consciousness by including Chaos and the emergence from Chaos as constitutive of any of its elements.

The artistic image expresses the final outcome of consciousness by same.

Consciousness is a lattice work of possibilities sometimes containing intentionality. To be conscious for example of the possibility of God's existence is to constitue such possibility within a network of value and responsibility which includes Chaos.

No negatives exist. Everything that exists, including absence, is irradiated by fundamental presence. The use of such concepts as zero and nothingness attempt to fixate value responsibly within the possibility for a Regime of Chaos.

The esthetic value of Zero may be said to contain the God as The Other Self. Since God is that sublimity that need not exist. Esthetics pertain to the *Aestheton*, the sensible. The *Noaestheton*, the nonsensible, pertains to paranoia [paranoia is that which exists alongside the nonsensible, i.e., that part of what is sensible (what exists) derived from what "should" not be sensible].

Esthetic value is based only on that which may be apprehended by our senses, therefore, to apprehend with our senses specifically that which evades our senses (as the concepts of Zero, God, or nothingness or paranoia do) indicates grace. Grace is defined along the lines of difference (what is or is not graceful), also of pure excrescence, of that which abnormally exceeds the limits of style; therefore decision, freedom and responsibility compose their own limit, since grace exceeds its origin, comes from somewhere else. The interstitial, multi layered matrix including Zero, Grace, God, Chaos and nothingness or paranoia includes conceptual structures that only come into existence as a result of attention, (especially paranoia). Of conscious, intentional hypercharging of an ideal state, a concept, an ideality.

Memories only come into being as we choose to recall them or not. Yet they only exist insofar as we remember them, or imagine them. Poetic discourse provides an aspect of imagination that is purely productive (that is to say, the poetic image could not be derived without force). Yet one that is original, too (in both senses of uniqueness and origin).

The poetic image hypercharges language, making each word's emanation field, the fixed structure that emanates from the fixed center point, the word, fuel the unified charge, the text (by separating itself from other, unique words, and also by linking those separations into a unified thing). The text, the unified charge, in turn fuels each emanation field, each word (by separating itself from other texts, and also by linking those separations into a language, a textual, neutronic field).

Letters are atoms, their emanation fields link to form single neutronic fields of words, words with texts, and texts with language. Language is the neutronic field, but also an emanation field which links with other emanation fields, like consciousness, to make other neutronic fields, like identities.

Yet memories may force themselves upon us. And this happens when we read. When we enter into a discourse with any Other, since reading constitutes the discourse of an Other (even if it is, only language). The Chaos which pools all possibilities within a presence of dynamic change (the absolute continuation of the world's existence included) provides the background for competing interests in the space of consciousness, while remaining one such interest. We have fundamental presence as constitutive of memory, and selection as its sometime articulation.

Psychosis is not selective, yet mnemopsychosis is, because it includes fundamental presence, memory, within a movement of hypercharging, which can only exist in consciousness. Even if memories force themselves into our consciousness, we are still responsible for their articulations, while if thoughts relating to things other than what we remember force themselves into our minds (as happens in psychosis) we can find the responsibility elsewhere.

What interests me is the difference between the thoughts of what does happen and what does not.

It is similar in structure to the difference between the juridical subject (made to stand in a political setting and articulate the degree to which it is responsible for its own existence, thereby helping to officiate that existence consciously and in the presence of an Other whose testimony may be compared to his own) and the radically free subject (who is able to access either the probability or possibility of Pure Exteriority, as in drugs or ecstasy or possession, or regression/progression of the Soul, and who is not even necessarily forced to exist, as in God). These structures are included in the universal matrix structure grid.

STANLEY GEMMELL
1/14/00

Thanks To Terry Skrinjar for the new physics.

Anergy: The hypothesis interpreting sensations in terms of the infinite phases of negative energy, which is motion less than zero. (Montague)

Aeviternity: (Lat. aevum, never-ending time) Eternity conceived as a whole, apart from the flux of time; an endless temporal medium in which objects and events are relatively fixed.

Aetiology: (Gr. aitiologeo, to inquire into) An inquiry into causes. Etiology: (1) The science or philosophical discipline which studies causality; (2) The science of the causes of some particular phenomenon, e.g. in medicine the science of the causes of disease.

Printed in the United States
by Baker & Taylor Publisher Services